THE DEPTHS
of
MY Soul

AuthorHouse™
1663 Liberty Drive
Bloomington, IN 47403
www.authorhouse.com
Phone: 1 (800) 839-8640

Because of the dynamic nature of the Internet, any web addresses or
links contained in this book may have changed since publication and may
no longer be valid. The views expressed in this work are solely those
of the author and do not necessarily reflect the views of the publisher,
and the publisher hereby disclaims any responsibility for them.

This book is printed on acid-free paper.

ISBN: 978-1-7283-6122-2 (sc)
ISBN: 978-1-7283-6123-9 (e)

Print information available on the last page.

Published by AuthorHouse   05/14/2020

authorHOUSE®

ANJA LEUENBERGER

THE DEPTHS OF MY SOUL

About the Author

My name is Anja Leuenberger I was born in Switzerland. When I was 14teen years young I was discovered as a model. I've always wanted to travel the world. I was shy and introverted because I was bullied in school. So, when the opportunity occurred, I took it. Signed a contract with my first agency. I've finished school and worked as a business women before full time traveling the world. I had a rough start in the industry, I was insecure and took every opinion personal. I am 27 now, living in New York and happy to say that I've had a very successful career already. Through this industry I learned to speak up and set boundaries for myself. Now that I made myself a name, I felt called to use it for more.

About the book

I have experienced sexual assault in my industry at a young age
multiple times. Unfortunately, till this day, it's unclear to people
what consent means. I was raped 2 times before my twenties, and it
made me stronger than my younger me could ever believe. I was young,
I was broke. It took me years to even find it within me to speak.
I was too ashamed. So, I started to write my deepest, scariest
thoughts down. I lost my voice for years. I lost myself. So here I
am, thanks to my poems. Vulnerable, stripped to my soul, giving you
a piece of me, my voice to find yours. To start your healing too. I
want to thank everyone who supported me in my process of healing.
Who gave me love support. And mostly didn't judge me when I opened
up. I hope this book gives you strength to find your voice, knowing
that with speaking up we can help each other.

Waking up to your weight on my chest

I am not able to breathe

not able to move

paralyzed by your face like it was yesterday

Reliving in my dreams

Will you ever leave

Will you?

-Trauma

Some secrets can haunt forever

Sometimes it's hard to find what happened within me to speak

As much as I want to scream

I just find myself lying here

Knowing that I will never be the same person anymore

-Secrets

Is it still rape if you can't seem to find
yourself screaming and kicking?

Or just a loss of energy to defend what
was taken a long time ago

-Survivor

Hate, a word so strange to me until you crossed my path

Hate, a word connected to your face

Hate, I can't seem to scrub you off no matter how hard I try

Something so sticky it won't come off

-You, The Man Who Raped Me

I try to deny it but a part of you
ruined something in man for me

You probably don't even know how present you still are in my life

-Trust Issues

I loved you for being you, just you, perfectly

All off a sudden you find yourself in pieces

Scared and vulnerable, afraid of what I will be thinking

I hold you, like no one held you before

And tell you, now your perfect not like before

And all you have to worry about, is that
I love you now, even more

Every single bits and pieces

-Imperfections

The cold touch of your hands woke me up

I try to catch my breath to scream your
hand already covers my mouth

Once again, the only thing to do is floating out of my own body

forced to watch from above

-Nightmares

Being a victim of sexual assault doesn't define me!

Being a survivor of sexual assault and
rape doesn't define who I am today

It plays a big role in who I am based on my unconsciousness,

influencing my daily behavior without me even knowing sometimes

But it's not who I am

It always will be a part of me, often it triggers me

It's like drowning in a sea of anxiety

But it passes and every time it does, I am stronger
better and most importantly getting it all out of me

-Cleansing

I tried to run away from you

Almost started hating you

The parts I once loved, being so far and strange

I tried to get rid of you because I thought this can't be you

But the time passed by and every once
more I stop and stare at you

I realized, honestly just want to be you

-My True Self

The strength of letting go without ever being apologized to

I forgive, not only once

but every damn time you try to be a part of my memory

-Forgiveness

Years pass by

And I always try

Silently I want to scream, want to ask for help

But look there is my pride

I love it makes me thrive

But often also makes me cave

-Pride

First it hurts then it's shameful but then it empowers

-Pain

Dear silence, you know me so well

caged me, but also made me feel so very safe

Bullies made me become your best friend

Because not speaking, did not make them seek me

Lingering for words to describe what's inside
me, but could never get it right

The world called my name I left,

And when I just started finding my voice again

Hands chocked me so hard, I didn't even know my own thoughts

Silenced once again, silenced by myself

Because if I didn't speak about it, it didn't exist

Oh Silence, I chose you for just a little too long

But the silence made me think, thoughts I didn't
know, far from the deepest I had or known

Piling up and up until they're are more than over the top

One day silence and I were trying to get up, collapsed
under the weight of the unspoken, oh silence

I scream, there is so much pain, scared of my
own body not being able to support

But in this moment, I realized, I screamed because
it's time to let go of the wrong support

Oh silence the time is here to let you go

Oh silence here we are one last time

Never wanting to cross you again

-Silence

I used to be afraid of silence and darkness

Day by day I would find my ways to make
the two never be a part of me

I danced with the air around the silence and darkness,
just like butterflies dance around nature

Smooth and effortless

Because being busy and occupied, so much
easier than facing reality

When I exchanged the flower with the world and
started dancing with the sun, moon and starts

I started to feel that silence and darkness can be so
much warmer, than dancing around it made me ever feel

I faced and payed attention

Like a burning meteor entering the
atmosphere, I started opening up

Warming up to the comfort and secrets these hold within,
and learned that they tell me more than the past ever has

Silence is full of wisdom; all you need to do is start to listen

-Healing/Trusting

The second I love, have joy and feel free

you somehow trigger my mind

making me believe that you are the person I love and want

playing like a movie in my mind

I start to cry and want to scream

you always take my breath when all I do is want to scream

I stay silenced

Now my partner is confused

he will never understand what just happened

-Sex Trigger Points

One day I will be able to close my eyes again

not being afraid of my dreams

One day I will be all in piece again

-One Day

Your words to me are the stitches to my scars

Every word has its own vibration

Vibration that surrounds me with love and comfort

The Stitches gain trust

Trusting that there is more than I thought there was

A certain trust I can't find words for

I want to say so many things, but I often get lost

Caught in the vibration, going along with the melody it builds

Surrounding me, holding me

We all deserve is love and trust

-Stitches To My Scars

I hold onto you with my fingertips

not sure if this is letting go or starting over

-Broken Heart

She described her first love with such an
ease, no signs of effort, just peace

Her eyes sparkled

Until this moment I thought diamonds were strong

It's a love story like never heard before

If you are really quiet, you can hear her heartbeat

Secretly everybody is guessing, who could this be

As she swings around the story of love and need

It's seems the only one she needed to meet
was no one else then her own needs

-Self Love

Because far away from a mile, knowing this
finding you definitely makes me smile

I believe in you, take care

When the soul is tired sleep doesn't help

-Dear Fighter

Oh little angel crying in my arms,

I wish I could help

I wish I could make you feel better

But sometimes not helping is the best way to help

Just being here holding you tight in my arms

Assuring you in a breaking world I am here and will never part

Like a nutrient tree I stand here, giving you shelter

No matter who did what to you, it will only ground you

Oh little angel don't worry

People always pay for their buried lies

-Little Angel

The way you walk in a room and light it up

Light it up so bright no matter how much
darkness is inside of you

I almost want to cry, of the beauty you carry

you carry all the time to cover the darkness

and only the souls who managed to slip
in my deepest of the heart

will ever know that all that light

wasn't always so bright

-Dear Mirror

Acknowledgments

Through darkness comes light. I deeply believe we sometimes experience bad, dark things in life in order to actually be led onto the path of light. Find guidance. Sometimes in order to gain we need to experience loss. I've experienced losing my true self, but not because I was raped, because I silenced myself. If there's pain, anxiety and fear in your body we don't talk about, it turns into physical pain. I didn't speak about what happened for almost 7 years. One day, I woke up, getting out of bed. I couldn't walk! My body didn't want to carry me anymore, my body was giving up on me. I crawled to a doctor, did x rays, saw several doctors and physicist. No one could help me. I had a huge wake up call. My body was trying to tell me something. TALK. Let it out. Stop holding in your anger, your pain and fear. So I started writing. And through the writing I eventually started speaking up. Finding that people actually understand and want to help you. But my fear of being judged and the shame held me back for years. This is why I deeply wanted to publish this book. For a while actually, but it took me courage, courage I knew other souls out there need. Because once I started talking about it, I only realized, to how many of us this happens every day.

So I jumped my fear and laughed at it while putting on my helmet of strength. And I said to myself people out there need to read this. They need to know they are not alone. It took me a good 3 years of intense Pilates and workouts, finding love for my body to heal. This is only going to make you so much stronger, than who did this to you will ever be. So here I am speaking up, I found my voice, and if I can I want to be yours.

A big thank you to Samantha Pell, my Pilates trainer. She helped me heal my body, together with my soul. And strengthens it to this day. Thank you for being my guardian angel on earth. And my entire family for loving me. Thanks to Ronja, Oliver, Muriel and Thuli for being some of my longest and strongest friendships.

When we hit rock bottom and darkness, the only thing that can save us are our thoughts. Because they vibrate through the body. I didn't only heal through talking about what happened, but by loving myself and being grateful, by raising my vibration. We all continue to heal every day. Let's heal and love together. Be a voice for others. And help them raise their vibration.

Printed in the United States
By Bookmasters